UMPIRING IN THE LITTLE LEAGUE

By MORRIS A. SHIRTS & KENT E. MYERS
With the help of Klien Rollo

S STERLING PUBLISHING CO., INC. NEW YORK

OTHER BOOKS BY THE SAME AUTHOR

Playing with a Football — Shirts & Kingsford
Warm Up for Little League Baseball — Shirts

CALL
IT RIGHT!

Contents

Before You Begin 7

The Umpire 9
   The Character of the Umpire . . . Dependability . . .
   Dress Standards . . . Special Equipment for Umpires . . .
   Firmness, Friendliness and Fairness . . . Knowledge and
   Training

The Umpire's Signals 21
   The Voice of the Umpire . . . Hand Signals

Positioning and Responsibility 33
   The Chief Umpire . . . The Chief Umpire Plus One . . .
   The Chief Umpire Plus Two . . . The Chief Umpire Plus
   Three

Field Decorum 59
   Before the Game Begins . . . Ground Rules . . . Handling
   the Players . . . Handling Coaches . . . Handling Fans
   . . . Handling Scorekeepers . . . Ending a Ball Game . . .
   Protesting a Ball Game . . . Preventative Umpiring

Troublesome Rules and Difficult Calls 79
   The Infield Fly . . . The Balk . . . Leaving the Base Too Soon
   . . . Spectator Interference

Call It Right! 86

Index 96

Before You Begin

Baseball is a game that has to be played by the rules, and every rule has a reason for being in the book. The umpire must know these rules better than anyone else on the field, as his decision and interpretation of the rules often make the difference between winning and losing, and between good field decorum and wild chaos.

Umpires need to cultivate a positive image of respect, fairness, firmness, and friendliness. Little League baseball players should look upon the umpire as a friend whom they can trust and respect. And so the umpire needs to learn how to be a friend to them, remain firm, though not ferocious and unbending. The umpire should also look at the Little League baseball player as a a child, not a small adult, and realize that he is learning citizenship and sportsmanship as well as baseball.

As you are reading this book, assume you are an umpire in a very crucial game. How would you rule on the hypothetical situations given before each chapter? During a summer of baseball, each is likely to occur. The correct answers to the situations begin on page 86, together with the reference to the Little League rule and the reason behind the decision. Please keep in mind that these situations are based on the rules used by Little League Baseball Inc., and may not apply to all of the hundreds of other different baseball organizations, nor to adult or professional baseball.

Call it Right!

Situation 1: A pitcher attempts a throw to first base, then steps back on the rubber as if to make the next pitch. The runner is then tagged out by the first baseman who has kept the ball hidden in his mitt. Is the runner out?

Situation 2: An umpire calls "infield fly" as the ball is hit in the air near the baseline to an infielder. However, the ball drops untouched to the ground and rolls into foul territory before passing first base. What happens?

(See page 86 for solutions.)

The Umpire

In Little League baseball, as in professional baseball, one of the most important factors in setting the "tone" of the game is the attitude and performance of the umpire. He affects the mood of the fans, the players and the coaches. This is especially true of volunteer umpires. In the Little League the umpires are volunteers, as are all other participating adults, and as volunteers, represent the spirit of the game as well, since they feel it important enough to give their time without monetary compensation. What kind of a person should the umpire be? What are the desirable characteristics he should bring to the game?

The Character of the Umpire

One of the first things to look at is the moral character of the umpire. The "village bum" cannot umpire a baseball game effectively—even if he knows the rules better than anyone else in the community. Umpires, managers, coaches and other adults working with the program should be models of good behavior, both on and off the field. A respectable businessman, the mayor, a religious leader or a city councilman would usually qualify and serve well as a Little League umpire, if his personal life and behavior are on a par with the mores of the community. On the other hand a man or woman whose moral habits are suspect would be a poor risk.

Like teachers, adults working in the Little League Baseball Program are frequently used by youngsters as models of behavior. Most children of Little League age are in a "hero-worship" stage, and they consciously or unconsciously mimic

9

and emulate the actions, language, and attitudes of those around them. This imitation may include hair and dress styles, mannerisms, body movements, and general attitudes toward manhood, womanhood, citizenship, religion, and ideals. There is more of a tendency for youngsters to transfer their loyalties to their coach or manager than to the umpire. Still, the way that young people react to the umpire and to authority in general can be more than casually affected by the way the umpire behaves. A high school graduate of questionable character who has never played baseball or an adult picked at random from a crowd would not and could not demand the respect of boys and girls, coaches, or fans, as much as someone who has a good reputation and who is known to be honest and fair.

With the current attitudes and behavior of crowds toward sports officials, this desirable type of umpire is getting increasingly hard to find. The current trend may never be reversed, at least not for a long time, unless we can get the right adults working with young people in their developmental stages. We need men and women of the highest moral and spiritual values working with our young people, and this includes baseball umpires!

Dependability

An umpire has to be absolutely dependable and on time. There is no such thing as being dependable "most" of the time. It is distracting and unnerving to players and coaches to be ready to get the game under way and not have an umpire. Players get nervous, coaches get angry, pitchers get cold, and fans become irritable.

It is not enough for an umpire to show up just as the game is scheduled to begin. He must be there early. All participants need to be aware that the umpire is there and that things are well organized and well in hand. Pre-game discussions need to take place. The umpire needs to go over the ground rules, check the condition of the field, the game equipment and safety problems on the field. (If a player is injured during a game due to an unsafe field condition, the blame can and should be placed directly on the umpire if he failed to notice the problem before the game began.) He needs to check the rosters and the batting orders, and see that the scorekeepers have their books ready.

It seems trite even to mention these points to anyone who has ever worked with baseball games, but we still have undependable umpires who are late and not properly ready to begin the game.

While it is most important that the umpire be at the field

This umpire is poorly dressed and might not command the respect of coaches and ball players.

A neat, well-dressed umpire inspires confidence and respect.

early to get things well in hand, he must also remain on the job for the entire game, and stay afterwards to close it down properly. His job does not end when the game is over. He still has duties to perform in bringing the game to a successful conclusion. Aside from everything else that has been said, being early and staying until after the players leave gives the impression that the umpire is sincerely interested in the game and the players.

Dress Standards

The way an umpire dresses can and does have an effect on the mood of the fans, the players, and the coaches at a baseball game. If an umpire appears on the field dressed in cut-off pants, a "T" shirt, and tennis shoes, he generates a certain unbecoming attitude and is perceived to lack experience. On the other hand, if the umpire is dressed in a clean, traditional uniform, he generates a feeling of confidence.

The uniform need not be expensive, but it must be neutral in color. Generally speaking, it should consist of a dark shirt, pants, shoes and a regulation umpire cap. Usually the color is blue, so as not to be confused with the colors typically found in baseball uniforms. Some umpires prefer to wear a white shirt with a dark tie. This is usually acceptable since the all-white shirt with a dark blue tie is easily differentiated from player uniforms. If the league does not furnish caps, umpires should purchase their own. In some circles it is said that "clothes make the man," and this is true in large measure for baseball umpires. Well dressed, the umpire is seen to be an "official."

Do not wear glasses, if you can see without them. At no time should an umpire wear dark glasses.

It would be most helpful if league officials would adapt a standard of dress for umpires. In that event, the above guidelines would be applicable.

Special Equipment for Umpires

The baseball league should purchase the special equipment needed by umpires. This includes (1) a mask, (2) a chest protector, (3) shin guards, (4) a ball sack, (5) a balls-and-strikes counter, and (6) a small whisk broom. Shoes with steel toe caps are recommended for plate umpires but they are not absolutely necessary. However, they must not have cleats or spikes. (In addition, men are advised to wear an athletic supporter and a cup. Women need no other special equipment, unless they prefer a special padded bra, but this is at their own discretion.)

To ask umpires to work without this protective equipment is to ask them to risk certain injury. We are speaking, of course,

(Left) A balls-and-strikes counter should be used by the plate umpire, although field umpires can also use them as a double check. (Right) The ball sack is usually attached to the plate umpire's belt. Keep spare balls in it so that the game is not delayed by out-of-play balls.

Both the face mask and the chest protector are essential equipment for the plate umpire. This umpire is wearing a pneumatic (inflatable) protector.

about the umpire who works behind the plate. Field umpires would not need the mask, chest protector, shin guards nor the whisk broom, but they might well carry a counter and use it to back up the plate umpire. They might even find use for a ball sack (to keep stray balls) although it is not necessary.

Chest protectors can be worn under or over the clothing. Some Major League umpires wear protectors under their coats and, unless one is especially looking for it, they are not noticeable. The "padded" protector is commonly used and can be worn inside or outside the clothing. However, neither padded protector offers as much protection as the pneumatic type, which

15

Use a whisk broom to keep home plate clean and free of dirt.

can be blown up by means of a rubber valve, like an air mattress, and then deflated for storage. The pneumatic chest protector is a little more difficult to wear as it is loose fitting so that it can be taken off easily and quickly. Consequently, it has to be held in place by the arms and hands when you are bent over.

Shin guards are worn under the pants legs and are designed to protect the upper arch of the foot, the ankle and the lower leg. Worn outside the pants legs, they would look cumbersome and would be distracting. Under the pants leg they are unseen and unnoticed, and do not provide any distraction from the game.

The *ball sack* is standard and designed so that it can be attached to the belt loop, or tied around the waist. It should be the same color as the uniform so it won't be distracting.

Firmness, Friendliness and Fairness

The umpire, in all his words and actions, should demonstrate that he is firm and impartial, but helpful as well. The umpire who maintains an attitude of friendly firmness will be accepted by young players as someone who can help them play ball better.

You can be firm without being unbending or unyielding. As the umpire, you must insist on complete observance of the rules, and be firm in your interpretation of those rules. But this does not mean that you cannot change your mind if a mistake has been made. In such cases, you must remain impartial.

For example: A runner comes into home plate, and from where the umpire is standing, it looks as if the catcher missed the tag. The umpire calls the runner "safe." On a second look, the umpire sees the runner doubled up with pain and asks the boy, "Did that catcher touch you?" The boy says, "Yes! Right in the stomach!" The umpire then changes his mind and calls the boy "out." Of course, the runner's manager comes running out of the dugout with a "bee in his bonnet." The umpire remains firm and simply says, "I missed the tag. He was tagged in the stomach and he is out!" In this case the umpire was firm and fair.

The umpire must not be partial. Sometimes this is difficult to accomplish. Many times in Little League we see the father of a boy on one of the teams serving as an umpire, which is unfortunate. This umpire may very well be impartial, but he may be accused of being partial when actually he bends over backwards to give the other team the advantage, rather than make an accurate and close call favoring his son's team.

On one occasion, when the son of the plate umpire was the pitcher, the son claimed after the game that his dad was not "giving him the corners." The father admitted it. "Son, I couldn't give you the corners, the crowd would have been against me!''

This situation should never be permitted! Fathers who have boys on a team should not umpire when that team is playing. When asked to umpire in a situation where partiality might be claimed, be honest and decline the assignment courteously, on the grounds that it would be difficult for you to be impartial and fair. Even when both managers and teams agree, unforeseen circumstances can develop to the detriment of all concerned.

The umpire should be absolutely certain of his "call," and then remain firm about it. Being firm, fair, and friendly does not mean that the umpire can be made to change a decision or that he is a push-over! However, if an honest mistake is made, the umpire is duty bound to reverse the decision. (It is bad to do this when calling "balls" and "strikes," and it is a clear admission of negligence if you constantly change your mind on these types of calls.) When it is a case of not knowing a rule, or of misinterpreting a rule, the umpire would not be fair if he was not to change his decision.

Young ball players should develop a healthy respect and admiration for umpires. They should have confidence in the umpire and know that he has made the right call. The young player should not live in mortal fear of the umpire, but rather think of him as a friend who is there to administer the rules fairly, and in whom he can confide and get help in learning the rules and so become a better ball player.

Knowledge and Training

There are only two ways you can learn to become an umpire: through experience and through study. Preferably, both should be involved.

Adults past the age of active participation must study, but

this should be tempered with indirect involvement of some type. The best way, next to being an active player, is to become an avid fan, watching as many games as possible, and trying to apply the rules as if you were an active player or umpire. To have been, at one time or another, an active participant takes an element of suspicion out of the minds of players, coaches, and adults. Obviously, it is more difficult to become a good umpire if you have never played the game. It is possible to become a good umpire by reading the rules alone, but that's hardly the desirable way to do it. Women, especially, should go the extra mile to become well trained. Until the sex barrier is completely broken, an element of distrust may still linger in the minds of the current crop of players, coaches, and fans.

Even when umpires are knowledgeable from training and experience, more is needed. Every league should have an "umpires' school" before the season begins. Rules are constantly changing in the Little League, and these changes should be studied carefully. The best way to do this is in a group. In addition, the general attitude, posture, behavior, and philosophy for umpiring in the league should be thoroughly studied and explained so that the entire umpire corps can operate in the same fashion.

Call It Right!

Situation 3: The batter steps out of the batter's box just as the pitcher goes into his pitching motion. The pitcher stops his pitching motion. What does the umpire do?

Situation 4: A batter hits several foul balls in succession just out of the reach of the right fielder, who tries vainly to catch them. The defensive coach calls time out and moves the right fielder into foul territory, hoping to get him into a better position to catch the next foul ball knocked there. What decision should the umpire make?

(See page 86 for solutions.)

The Umpire's Signals

There are eleven basic "calls" or signals an umpire uses. Usually only one involves a voice call (given by the umpire behind the plate when he calls a strike). The rest are given physically with the arms or hands.

The Voice of the Umpire

The voice that an umpire uses to announce his decisions is a good indicator of his attitude and confidence. Few things are more annoying and generate more distrust among players than an umpire who under his breath announces his decision meekly. You do not need to put on a circus act when you make a decision, but use a loud voice and accompany your call with the appropriate gesture.

It seems ridiculous, but one umpire attributed his success on the field to the fact that he practiced making calls at home in a closet with his head in a laundry bag! Umpires' calls should be firm, loud, and distinctive. Another thing to remember about an umpire's voice is that it should not be used to belittle a player, especially the hitter. Your prime responsibility is to make your decision clear to everyone concerned.

Hand Signals

1. Balls and Strikes. When announcing a decision from behind the plate on balls and strikes, it is usually not necessary to call out the "balls." In general, if no "call" is made, the pitch was a "ball."

Strikes are something else. The strike call should be bellowed

"Strike One" is the call. Your vocal call should be loud and the gesture of the right hand should be unambiguous. **No motion is needed if the pitch is a ball.**

loudly, accompanied with an appropriate and consistent physical gesture. (It is best if the word "strike" is pronounced in two syllables with the emphasis on the first syllable, like this: "stee-rike." If the strike call is announced in a normal tone using a normal pronunciation, it would get lost in the crowd noise.) The physical gesture is usually made with the right hand in a closed fist position, with the arm extended as if to pull down on a rope. Another accepted gesture is to move the right hand laterally, and away from the plate. Many umpires feel their chief obligation is to the scorekeeper, but if your signals and voice are distinctive and easily heard, you will eliminate frequent inquiries from managers and coaches to whom, for strategic reasons, the calls must be plainly given.

The remaining calls made by umpires are mostly physical, although accompanying verbal signals are also used for emphasis.

2. The Out. The universal signal for an "out" is given with a clenched fist with the thumb out. Use a short, upward and

Indicate an "out" by jerking your right hand up. Your fist should be clenched, with the thumb out.

(Above) This umpire has called a runner safe. His arms are extended, with the palms facing the ground. (Left) "Time" is called by the umpire. Move two or three steps toward the infield when making this call.

A balk has been called against the pitcher. Step toward the pitcher as you make this call.

outward movement of the wrist and forearm. An "out" can be called by any umpire—the chief umpire or any of the field umpires. The signal must be given immediately and quite vigorously, leaving no question that the "out" has been called.

3. Safe. Given with both hands extended with the palms down, the "safe" movement usually begins with both hands in front of the chest. Then, fling them out toward the play. Hold your hands in position long enough for all to see.

4. Time. Extend the right arm to the front, the palm facing forward and the fingers up. This signal looks like a traffic patrolman signaling traffic to stop or halt. The umpire usually takes two or three steps toward the infield when giving the time signal so all can see it. This is especially true when it is given by the plate umpire.

5. Balk. (For an explanation of a "balk," see page 81.) Any umpire can make this call. It is called against the pitcher and is given by raising the extended arm fully to the front, the fist clenched with the knuckles toward the pitcher. Like the "time" call, the umpire should take a step or two toward the infield. In certain circumstances a balk may be ignored. If, for example, the pitcher delivers the ball and the batter gets a good hit, a committed balk would probably not be called.

6. *Interference.* Called when a base runner interferes with the defensive player as he attempts to catch or throw the ball, this signal is made by raising the right arm over the head. Keep the forearm parallel to the ground and the hand palm down. Raise and lower the hand to the head or cap several times.

7. *Obstruction.* When a fielder obstructs the progress of a base runner, the umpire indicates the infraction by placing both hands on his hips, raising and lowering them several times.

Interference by a base runner is indicated by raising and lowering the right arm over the head.

Obstruction is called on a fielder if he impedes the progress of a base runner. Raise and lower your hands to your hips to signal this call.

Indicate that a fly ball is "fair" or "foul" by motioning with both hands in the direction that the ball has traveled—toward the playing field if the ball is fair, or away from the playing field if the ball is foul.

8. Foul or Fair Ball. A "foul ball" is different from a "foul tip." A foul ball is usually a hard hit ball that leaves the playing field outside of the base paths or over the backstop. Many times it is difficult for all participants to see a foul ball, and it becomes essential that the umpire call the play as early and as distinctly as possible. The call is given by raising both hands above the head, palms out, and motioning in the direction in which the ball has gone or landed. If the motion is to the outside of the playing area, the ball is foul. If the motion is in the direction of the playing area, it indicates a fair ball.

9. Foul Tip. When the hitter just barely ticks the ball with the bat, and the catcher misses the foul ball, the umpire signals a foul tip. Play stops immediately on a foul tip and therefore the umpire must give a distinctive call. All players must understand that this has happened, as runners cannot advance on a

Indicate a foul tip immediately by crossing both arms above your head, striking your right wrist with your left hand.

foul tip. Give the signal by crossing both arms above the head with the left hand striking the right wrist several times.

29

Field umpires usually make the call if a runner leaves his base too quickly, before the pitched ball crosses the plate. Drop a flag (red is preferred) if you spot an infraction.

10. Leaving the base too soon. This is a rule peculiar to Little League. A base runner may not leave a base before the pitched ball crosses home plate. If an infraction occurs, it is indicated by dropping a red flag (or a flag of any color) as soon as the infraction is seen. Field umpires are usually the ones to make this call and they should have a red flag as part of their umpiring equipment.

11. Walk. The plate umpire indicates that the hitter has "drawn a walk" by fully extending his right hand and arm toward first base.

This same gesture may also be given by an umpire when awarding a runner an extra base, a hit batter first base, or when ejecting a player, coach, or manager from the game.

When a batter is hit by a pitched ball, the ball is "dead." The umpire should immediately signal for a time out and check the physical condition of the batter. The umpire's first con-

Indicate a walk by extending your right arm toward first base.

sideration is the safety of the ball player. The hit batter is then awarded first base, and the game resumes if the umpire is satisfied that the batter was hit unintentionally.

Call It Right!

Situation 5: A manager comes from the dugout and goes directly toward his pitcher with a hand raised, palm out, while telling the umpire, "time!" What is the ruling? Can he do it?

Situation 6: A pitcher is having trouble getting the ball over the plate. His coach makes several trips to the baseline to talk with him. On his fourth such trip, the opposing coach demands that the pitcher be taken out as a pitcher. What would be your decision?

(See page 88 for solutions.)

Positioning and Responsibility

Umpiring in Little League is in some aspects different from umpiring in other baseball games, since some of the rules have been modified to allow for the age of the players and to foster a feeling of good sportsmanship and fairness. The essential difference lies in the fact that Little League involves young people. Umpires need to keep this constantly in mind and they must consider Little Leaguers as young people, and not small adults.

Four umpires (a chief umpire and three field umpires) are the ideal number to work a game, although it may not always be possible to have a full complement. How do the umpires work? Who is in control? Who takes which responsibility? Does one official handle everything?

The Chief Umpire

The chief umpire, the plate umpire, is the most important official on the field. How well he does his job determines the tone of the entire ball game. What are his duties and how does he discharge them efficiently and effectively?

1. He superintends the game. The chief umpire controls the conduct of the ball game. He makes all the pre-game arrangements. He must check that the team rosters and batting orders are properly submitted; that the field is in a good and safe playing condition; that each team can field nine eligible

This umpire is asking for trouble, umpiring behind the plate without a mask. He is, however, in an excellent position to call balls and strikes.

players; that the field is properly marked; and that the other officials are ready. He gets the ball game under way on time, sees that it is conducted properly and makes certain it is terminated correctly.

All other umpires and officials work under the direction and supervision of the chief umpire. He has the power to overrule the decisions of the other umpires (but usually doesn't without calling for a confidential conference with them which may result in the reversal of a decision).

The position of the chief umpire behind the plate is also a "command post" from which he can control the tone of the ball game and keep the tempo of the game from slowing unnecessarily. As the last out of the inning is made, the chief umpire should take a couple of steps into the infield, remind the players to "hustle," and encourage the pitcher to get his warm-up pitches under way. This shouldn't become routine or automatic as it can be irritating to the players and coaches and might even have the opposite effect.

2. Calling balls and strikes. In addition to his responsibility as the "umpire-in-chief," probably the next most important duty of the plate umpire is to call the balls and strikes. Except in rare circumstances, the best position to do this is right behind the catcher, working as closely to him as possible without touching or interfering with him.

The chief umpire cannot be timid or "gun-shy" of the baseball. He must watch the ball closely as it leaves the pitcher and reaches its destination—the catcher's glove or its flight from

This umpire is standing a bit too far behind the catcher and would have some difficulty making a call on a low pitch.

Use the fingers on your left hand to indicate the number of balls, and the fingers on your right hand to show the number of strikes. In this case the hitter has run up a count of 2 balls and 2 strikes.

the bat. He can't close his eyes on foul tips. He must be alert and know where the ball is *at all times*. Did it hit the bat? What part of the bat? Did it hit a player? On the hand? The arm? The shoe? He must have the concentration to avoid blinking or ducking when the ball gets by the catcher and comes toward him with terrific speed and force.

The best position for the chief umpire is directly behind the plate and close to the catcher. If he stands back too far, his view of the ball is obstructed by the catcher and he can't see the "corners" of the strike zone. Under this circumstance, the umpire can only guess if the ball crosses the boundary lines of the strike zone. His calls will be inaccurate and inconsistent and keep the catcher, pitcher, manager, fans and other players in a constant uproar. Good pitchers who have mastered some degree of control get upset if they aren't "given the corners." It isn't long until confidence is lost in the umpiring, which can lead to a potentially dangerous "loss of control" of the ball game as the innings progress.

Calling the balls and strikes accurately and consistently contributes a great deal in establishing the tone of a ball game. This can only be done well from a position directly behind and close to the catcher. Of course, this position is impossible to maintain if the umpire is not provided with special protecting equipment, including a face mask, chest protector, shin guards, athletic supporter and cup (for men), and possibly steel-toed shoes (as described on page 14). The absence of this equipment is the only justification for having the chief umpire stand on the mound behind the pitcher. This second position is at best a

The count on the batter is 3 balls and one strike. Players and coaches must know the count if they are to play the game well.

Show that the hitter has a "full count" against him (3 balls and 2 strikes) by holding up both fists closed rather than using your fingers.

compromise for the safety of the chief umpire and should not be used if it can be avoided.

3. Calling foul and fair balls. The chief umpire, working from behind the plate, is in the best position to determine whether a ball driven down either base line is fair or foul. This is a call the chief umpire should make. To do this, he should step in front of the plate, hold both hands high above his head, palms out, and signal away from the playing field if the ball is foul, and toward the infield if it is fair. Make this decision immediately or as soon as possible. Sometimes umpires wait until the ball lands outside the playing area before making a decision. This is wrong. If a ball is fair as it passes over the fence, it is a fair ball (and a home run) and the signal should be given immediately.

4. Making calls at the plate. When a runner attempts to score from third base, the chief umpire must make the call. No other umpire on the field is in a position to do it. The chief umpire must be conscious of the fact that a runner is on third and may

A close call at home! Does the catcher have the ball? Will he tag the runner out before the runner touches the plate? The plate umpire must be on top of the play to make the call.

You must be alert at all times and not carried away by the action in another part of the field. Did this runner miss home plate?

Move to one side to make calls at the plate. Stay close enough to see the action, but remember that you must not be so close as to interfere with the play. In this case the runner is safe, as the catcher has dropped the ball.

be planning to score. As the play develops, he must move away from his normal position near the rear of the plate so as not to interfere with the action, and yet be close enough to see if a tag is properly made, and if the runner touches the plate. He has to be "on top" of the play if the call is to be made correctly.

Another call the chief umpire frequently makes at the plate is the "balk." However, certain kinds of balks can be detected more easily by one of the field umpires. In these cases one of them should make the call.

Help from the field umpires may also be needed if the hitter "checks" his swing. When the rule was based on the position of the hitter's wrists, the chief umpire could frequently make this call without help. The rule now states that a strike is called if the bat crosses the front of the plate. If you are unsure of the call, check with the field umpire on third or first base to confirm your decision. But remember that the decision is yours to make.

5. Covering first and third. The chief umpire, from his position behind the plate, is in a good position to make calls at first and third base if he is working the game alone or in the event the field umpire is occupied with other calls. If, for example, the field umpire is busy making a call at second base and a runner is advancing to third, the umpire at home plate would probably be in the better position to make the call at third. Any time this type of a situation is likely to occur, the umpires must decide in advance who will make the call.

The Chief Umpire Plus One

At least one other umpire should be on hand to help the chief umpire, taking the responsibility to make most of the calls in the field. The position the field umpire takes depends upon the number of runners on the bases.

1. No runners on base. With no runners on base, the most likely play is at first base. This is called the "percentage" play. The ball might be hit to the outfield, requiring the judgment of the field umpire (for example, whether a fly ball is caught or trapped), but the most likely play will be on a ground ball thrown to first base. Therefore, the field umpire should take a position about 10 feet beyond first base in foul territory, enabling him to see the play while not interfering with it (see drawing). From this position, he will not interfere with the fielding of the ball, nor with the runner crossing the bag. It will also place him in the best position to judge whether the ball hits the mitt of the first baseman before the runner's foot

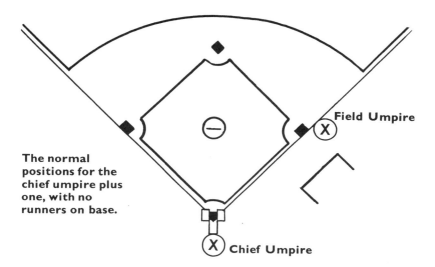

The normal positions for the chief umpire plus one, with no runners on base.

Field Umpire

Chief Umpire

This field umpire, though casually dressed, is in a good position to make the call at first. Watch the foot of the runner and listen for the sound of the ball hitting the first baseman's mitt to make the call.

43

This field umpire indicates clearly that the runner is out at first.

strikes the bag. He can also watch the action of the first baseman to see if he tags the runner.

2. Runner on first base. With a runner on first, things begin to
get a little complicated for the field umpire. He has two players
to watch. He needs to watch the runner on first, who can't
advance until after the pitched ball crosses the plate, and be
prepared to make the call as the runner advances to second.
He must also watch the batter as he tries to reach first base
safely. The "percentage" play is the play on second base, since
defensive teams will almost always try to "get the lead runner."
To prepare for this, the field umpire should take a position
nearer second base than first. Some umpires position themselves between the pitcher and second base. This is a logical
place in larger ball parks, but not on the small Little League
diamond. From such a position, the field umpire might

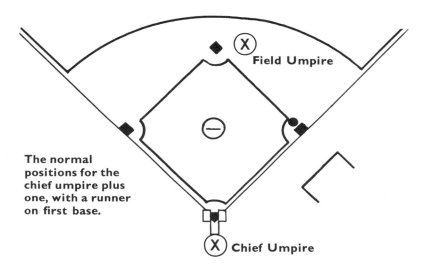

The normal positions for the chief umpire plus one, with a runner on first base.

Field Umpire

Chief Umpire

With a man on first, the "percentage" play is at second base. Move over from your normal position as the play develops so that you can make the call.

45

From the normal position, 10 to 15 feet behind and to the right-field side of second base, you can make the call on a fast-moving force play.

With no runners on base, this umpire has taken the wrong position.

46

interfere with a thrown or batted ball. It is especially difficult for a Little League catcher to make a throw over the field umpire to second base.

Since the field umpire's primary responsibility lies with making the call at second base, the best compromise position is a spot 10 to 15 feet behind the second baseman and a little to the right-field side (see page 45). As the play develops, the field umpire might need to move quickly toward second base to be "on top of the play" and thus make a more accurate "call."

Do not forget that first base is also the field umpire's responsibility. Usually, you should have no difficulty in making both calls, as they seldom happen simultaneously. However, the plate umpire, sensing that this could happen, should "cover" for the field umpire at first base by watching the runner advance to first. To avoid making simultaneous but different calls, the plate umpire should delay making any call on the bases to give the field umpire a chance to make it. If the field umpire hesitates, or appears to have missed the play, the plate umpire can give the call immediately.

3. Runner on second or runners on first and second. In this situation, there is some disagreement as to which position the field umpire should take. One school of thought holds that he should be stationed beyond second base, out of the play and a little toward the left-field side. This places him in an excellent position to watch the "percentage" play or to pick up an interference or obstruction play between second and third base. If the ball is hit toward the shortstop and hits the runner advancing to third base, or if the shortstop obstructs the advance of the runner, the field umpire could see it easily from this position. He would also be in a good position to make a call in case the runner gets caught in the "hot-box" between second and third.

In actual practice, however, it might be best for the field umpire to take his position behind second base and to the right-field side—the same position assumed when there is a runner only at first base (see drawing below).

The reasoning is easy to follow. The chances that a call would need to be made on the runner advancing to second are as great as they are for a runner advancing to third base. Since the plate umpire is in a relatively good position to make a potential call at third, it might be better for the field umpire to be on the right-field side of second base. From this position, he can make the call on the runner going into second, observe the runner on first to see if he left the base too soon, see an interference play centered around the shortstop area, and still possibly make the call on the runner going to first base. This would be especially true if he knew in advance that the plate umpire would be watching third base.

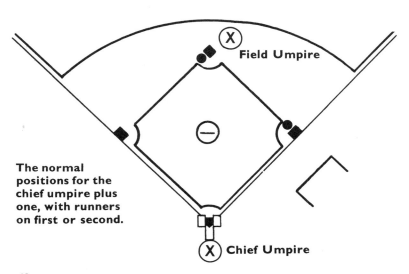

The normal positions for the chief umpire plus one, with runners on first or second.

The runner on first, having started for second, is now trying to return to first base. The field umpire had anticipated a play at second, but he is still in good position to call the play at first. He might need help from the plate umpire on the call since the play is close.

4. Runner on third base. There is also some disagreement among the experts as to where the field umpire should be placed when there is a runner on third base. Many feel he should be near third base in foul territory and a shade towards home plate. This places him in an excellent position for a "pick-off" play at third base, or a play where the runner on third must tag up for a fly ball. He is also in position to make a call on a close play at third on a runner advancing from second base. However, in taking this position, the importance of the play on the runner going to first base is overlooked. It is suggested that in this situation, it might be best to spot the field umpire behind first base, as is the case where there are

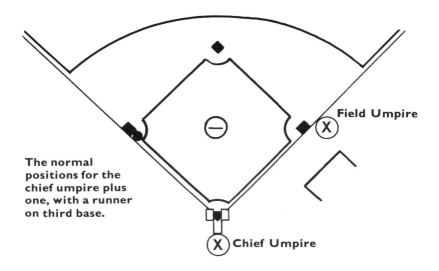

Field Umpire

The normal
positions for the
chief umpire plus
one, with a runner
on third base.

X Chief Umpire

no runners on base (see above). This, of course, would not
work unless the chief umpire in his position behind the plate
could make the call at third base. He needs to watch this
runner in any case because of the possibility of his advancing
to home plate.

The Chief Umpire Plus Two

Having two field umpires and a chief umpire improves the
quality of the umpiring considerably over the situation where
one field umpire and the chief umpire have to make all the
calls. The positions taken by two field umpires again change
according to the number of runners on base.

1. No runners on base—the "normal" position. If there is a
"normal" position it would be to place one umpire behind

On close plays especially, the field umpire's signal must be
immediate and unmistakable.

The third-base umpire can move quickly on the outfield side of the base path between second and third to make a call at second base or between second and third, or he can remain in his normal position to make the call at third.

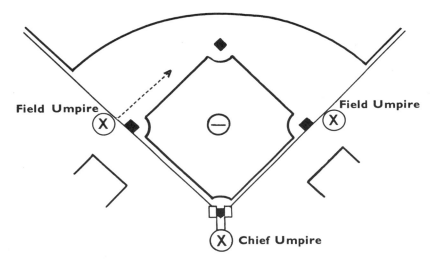

The normal positions for the chief umpire plus two, with no runners on base. The third-base umpire can move over easily to make a call at second.

first base and the other behind third base in foul territory and a little on the outfield side (see above). From this position an accurate call on the runner going to first base can be made. In the event that the hitter gets a double or a triple, the umpire behind third base can move quickly on the outfield side of the base path between second and third to make a possible call at second base. Or, he can maintain his position to make a possible call at third base on a triple.

2. Runner on any or all bases. With a runner on first base, an important call could develop either at first or second. Position one behind first base in regular fashion. From this position he can make the call on the batter advancing to first base. The

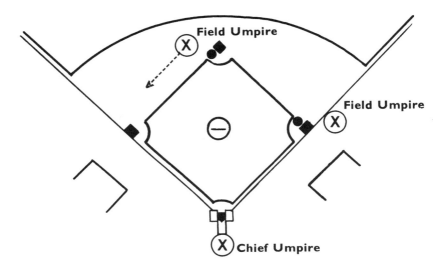

The normal positions for the chief umpire plus two, with runners on second or second and first. The umpire at second base can move over to cover the play at third.

other umpire should take up a position behind and between the shortstop and second base. From this position, he can make the call on a force play at second (see above). He is also in position to observe the action between second and third bases in case of a "hot-box," interference or obstruction play. He could also cover the play at third base if a play developed there.

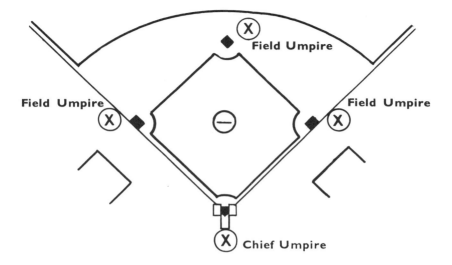

**The normal positions for a chief umpire plus three field umpires.
Each umpire is responsible for calls made at his base.**

The Chief Umpire Plus Three

The ideal arrangement is to have three field umpires—one for every base. They should each take the "normal" position. One should be behind and beyond first in foul territory, one should be behind second base on the right-field side, and one behind third base in foul territory. From these positions, they can cover all playing and fielding situations adequately. Each is responsible for making a call at his own base. Difficulties might arise in situations where simultaneous but different calls could be made. For example, one situation would involve making a call in a "hot-box" play between the bases. These difficulties

This third-base umpire is a bit too close to his base. However, since the fence is so close to the playing area, he has little choice.

This umpire has enough room to position himself to cover the play at third without becoming involved in the action.

can be avoided if it is understood that the umpire closest to the play is to make the call, and the other umpire is to remain quiet but available for consultation.

Call It Right!

Situation 7: A batter walks to the plate, takes his position in the batter's box and swings at the first pitch. The scorekeeper notices that he is batting out of turn and promptly notifies the umpire. The umpire calls the batter out. The coach of the boy objects. What does the umpire do?

Situation 8: Less than $3\frac{1}{2}$ innings have been played, the sun has gone down and darkness is settling in, and the umpire notices that the first baseman missed two easy ground balls he had been getting routinely. What should the umpire do?

(See page 88 for solutions.)

Field Decorum

Field decorum is that special feeling, atmosphere, aura, or spirit which adds color to a baseball game. It binds the players and the fans into a camaraderie which can ignite with a sudden explosiveness, carrying athletes to their greatest heights or deepest depths. The excitement of the game, the background noise of the crowd, the feelings between players on the field and between players and fans, the smell of hot dogs and popcorn; all help define field decorum. Much of it cannot be deliberately generated—it just happens.

At times, the atmosphere of a baseball game can become too charged with excitement, get out of hand and possibly lead to riot and injury. But most of the time, the atmosphere is positive, and it is one of the responsibilities of the umpire to keep it under control. This chapter is designed to help the umpire to discharge his responsibility in this area effectively.

Before the Game Begins

Under the direction of the umpire, managers exchange rosters and batting orders which are also given to the scorekeeper. This exchange establishes the official roster or batting order and eliminates arguments which could develop later in the game. As simple and as specific as this procedure sounds, it is violated almost daily on the Little League diamond, as very few umpires enforce this rule.

The proper procedure is to hold a formal meeting at home plate with the umpires and the managers of both teams. This formal meeting sets the tone of the game. Unfortunately, many managers send their batting orders to the scorekeepers with a team member. This gives the fans and players the impression that things are not in order, and that team and field officials are not speaking with each other. Because of this, the game could begin under a cloud of suspicion.

A meeting at the plate also gives the umpires and managers the opportunity to discuss problems, including any special ground rules or rule interpretations, that may need clarification before the game begins.

The obligations of the umpire do not begin with this meeting at the plate, which should be held only after he has taken care of some other important matters. The umpire should be at the ball park early, perhaps while the teams are warming up, to inspect the field carefully to see if it is in playable condition and ready to be used. If it is not, there may be time to repair it before the game begins.

Any possible problems which could affect the health and safety of the players should be identified. For example, if the groundskeeper has placed a steel support post near a seedling tree (a perfectly logical thing for him to do to protect the tree), it might pose a threat to the safety of a ball player chasing a fly ball. A collision by a player with such an obstruction could injure him, possibly seriously. This can be avoided by an alert umpire, who has the power to delay the game until the situation is corrected. Corners of sheet steel used to make the signs which sometimes adorn outfield fences might also be hazards for unsuspecting players chasing balls near the fence. An umpire may not discover all these potential dangers, but if no effort is made, a legal case of negligence could be made against the umpire or league officials. Some umpires have been observed picking up and tossing away rocks that they find on the playing field. This is a logical and commendable activity during the pre-game inspection.

A special ground rule might be needed to cover this fence, which is far too close to third base. Be sure you check all obstructions on or near the field to prevent injuries to the players. This umpire is not in a good position to call the play at third, since his view is blocked by the advancing runner. He should be closer to the play and nearer the fence.

The umpire should also note illegal articles of clothing or equipment worn or used by players and correct it during this period, rather than halt the game at a crucial moment. For example, a fielder warming up with a white or partially white mitt or a player with a white wrist band should be told it cannot be used once play begins, rather than cause a minor revolt by stopping him from entering the game with it.

An early arrival also gives the umpire a chance to visit with the players and coaches informally. During this time you might say things that would not be possible or appropriate during the game. Imagine the effect you could have on a young player if you said to him, "That was a great game you pitched the other day. That last ball you pitched was so close to being a strike, I was really hoping you could bring it across!'' You might even give him some advice that would be helpful to him.

This pre-game time can be used effectively to develop a desirable umpire image, if umpires would just use it.

Ground Rules

Every ball park has its idiosyncrasies, and may not even be the same today as it was yesterday. In most cases, special rules need to be made before the game begins to avoid misunderstandings later in the game. For example, the sprinkling system might have been left on, flooding the third base dugout,

Both boys and girls now play in the Little League. As an umpire, you can help them learn to work and play together.

in which case, the team occupying that dugout may have to be given permission to sit outside it. If a water hole has developed near second base, the umpire might want to establish a ground rule that all play halts if the ball lands in that spot. If part of the fence in left field has blown away during the night, a special rule might need to be established concerning balls going in that direction. (One league used a chain link fence which had curled up where the dogs crawled under it. During one game, a fielder chasing a ball caught his shoe in the fence at this spot, making it impossible for him to throw the ball he had fielded. A special ground rule was made to cover the problem in future games.) If the sky is dark and threatening, the umpire needs to discuss with both managers the possibility of having to call the game *before* the game begins.

These special problems involving ground rules, which might even be in contradiction to the rule book, need to be discussed and mutually agreed upon before the game begins.

Handling the Players

The ideal umpire-player relationship is one of mutual respect and trust. During the course of a closely fought ball game, tempers can flare. This is especially true with coaches and players, but it must never happen to the umpire. You are there to enforce the rules of the game and to keep it under control.

It is not the function of an umpire to belittle a ball player or a coach. Most of the time, it is better to ignore the sudden temper flashes of a young player and look for an opportunity to discuss it with him later. On the other hand, you must not permit constant verbal abuse by a young player. Yet even in these cases, it is much better not to deal directly with the player. It would be best to call time out and discuss the problem with his coach, privately and confidentially and with an attitude of firm compassion and concern for the desirable growth and development of the boy. Sometimes it becomes necessary to call time and take the player aside to discuss the problem as calmly as possible. Ejection from the game should be a last resort and used very sparingly. In any event, after the game is over, you should arrange a private meeting with the offended parties to discuss the situation.

Another dimension of the same problem occurs when you discern that a player is only reflecting the training received from the coach or manager. The player should not be punished for carrying out the orders of the coach. In this situation, you must deal directly with the coach, sometimes immediately, but it is better if postponed until tempers cool. Never bawl the coach out in front of the players. Abusive adult confrontations on the Little League baseball field should never be allowed. One general rule to remember is that it serves no good purpose to discipline or belittle someone in front of an audience. It is best done in private, or at least confidentially. Burning resentments develop as a result of public rebuke, can smolder under the surface for years, and then erupt in ways that are damaging to everyone concerned.

Handling Coaches

Much of what has been said about handling players is also appropriate when handling adults. As far as possible, you should ignore confrontations with coaches, simply turning your back on them or walking away from them. If the confrontation persists, you must hold your temper, and hope that someone intercedes before you are forced to eject the offender from the ball park.

Direct public confrontation between any adults on the Little League baseball field should be avoided. It serves no good purpose, and the umpire is in a position to do irreparable damage to the image of the offending adult. Many times opposing coaches yell at each other from the dugouts. This also should not be permitted. In this case, call time, get the two coaches together and simply tell them they are setting a bad example for the young players. You might also mention that it would be unfortunate if they had to be ejected from the game.

Occasionally, it is perfectly all right to call time and get the managers of each team together in the middle of the infield, or off to the side away from everyone else, to explain a decision, to discuss a possible impending infraction or for any other reason which could eliminate misunderstandings. It is better to talk problems out quietly rather than get into public shouting matches.

Handling Fans

Fans usually cause the most trouble at a Little League ball park. Most of them are parents who have a vested interest in each and every call you make. In adult baseball, disagreeing with the umpire seems to be a Great American Tradition—everywhere!—at least in the eyes of the fans. This should be kept at a minimum in the Little League. Of course, you cannot demand that the fans agree with you! But you can umpire in such a way that this disagreement is kept to a minimum. Respect must be earned!

There are some things you can and should do when it comes to fans. The fans must not be permitted to harangue or "razz" a Little League ball player. Unfortunately, this happens all too frequently. Men and women with loud voices sit in the stands right behind the plate, and browbeat the players as they come to the plate to take their turn at bat.

Fans also distract the pitcher with cat-calls, disparaging remarks, and uncouth language, sometimes to such a degree that playing baseball becomes a frightening experience.

One of the unfavorable aspects of Little League baseball is the intense emotional pressure placed on immature players. A player at bat, with the outcome of the game resting on his shoulders, experiences enough tension without having a loud-mouthed adult yelling at him from behind a screen. Likewise, a pitcher playing his heart out, sometimes almost in tears, doesn't need to hear derogatory remarks from the fans.

There are many who argue with this point of view, justifying themselves on the grounds that the players must face reality. Looking at it from the standpoint of developing a love for the game, gaining individual confidence, and learning sportsman-ship, there can be no place for such behavior in Little League baseball. If the players go on to high school, college and especially professional baseball, "Bronx cheers" should be expected. But little kids should not have to hear it at all!

What can you, as an umpire, do? Stop the ball game, and refuse to permit it to continue until the razzing stops. Have the offending adults removed from the stands. Foul and abusive language has no place in a Little League ball park, and it is the responsibility of all adults working in the program, especially the umpires, to see that it is stopped as soon as it begins!

Handling Scorekeepers

Scorekeepers sometimes forget who they are and try to take the game into their own hands. This is because they are not often aware of the extent (and limits) of their official function. Ideally, a chief scorekeeper is appointed for each game with at least one assistant scorekeeper. It is better to have two or three assistant scorekeepers, but the essential point is that one and *only one* of them can be the official scorekeeper.

Before the game begins, the umpire should go over the basic rules with the scorekeepers to make certain they are understood, and that only one chief scorekeeper is appointed. The chief scorekeeper must keep the scorebook accurately, and the umpire may check the official book from time to time to make certain that the game is being recorded correctly.

Frequently, each team has a scorekeeper, and both of them feel it essential to get the player rosters and changes directly from the managers of both teams. A frequent infraction is the manner in which the official roster and batting order is submitted. Unless he specifies otherwise, the official roster and batting order and any subsequent changes should be given to the chief umpire who, in turn, submits it to the chief scorekeeper. Frequently, the umpire will permit changes to be given directly to the chief scorekeeper, but the umpire should, in all cases, know that it has been done and properly recorded.

Scorekeepers play a silent role. Often, however, scorekeepers think it is their function to call the attention of the umpire, and sometimes the managers, to a player who is batting out of order. The penalty for batting out of order is being called out. It is *not* his duty. If the scorekeeper announces the infraction (sometimes over a loudspeaker), it draws the attention of the players and managers away from the game and takes authority away from the chief umpire. The *only* person on the field who can legally notify the umpire that a player is batting out of order is the manager or coach of the opposing team. If he calls it to the attention of the chief umpire, then, and only then, can the scorekeeper be brought into the picture. The scorekeeper's book must be in order and it must show that the player is definitely batting out of order. The chief umpire then has the obligation to call the batter "out."

Ending a Ball Game

The object of any ball game is to declare a winner. This must be done in each game unless, in your judgment, it would be detrimental to the health of the players to continue the game. If the game cannot be completed, it should be made up. If the players, fans and officials do not know the rules, a ball game can end in confusion.

Theoretically, there are only four ways a ball game can end: (1) as a regulation game; (2) as a regulation-drawn game; (3) as a suspended game; and (4) as a forfeited game. You should know the rules well enough to interpret the situation to the managers, coaches, players and other officials in such a way that they all know and understand what must be done and how to do it.

1. The regulation game. In Little League baseball, a regulation game is one in which a winner can be determined after 6 innings of play, unless the home team (which bats last) is ahead after $5\frac{1}{2}$ innings of play. In this case, the last half of the last inning is not played. If the game is called after four complete innings of play because of darkness or inclement weather, it is considered a regulation game. (Of course, the last half of the fourth inning need not be played if the home team is leading at that point.) If the game has to be called at any time after the end of the fourth inning, the score at the conclusion of the last full inning of play would determine the winner.

2. A regulation-drawn game. If the score is tied after the completion of four or more complete innings of play, and the umpire has to call the game due to darkness, inclement weather, or for some other reason which would make it unsafe to continue, the game must be rescheduled at a later date, with play resuming at the *exact* point it was terminated. This point should be noted in the score book. The scorekeeper uses the same score sheet, and the game is resumed as if it had never been interrupted. The batting order must be the same and substitutions are made as if it were a continuation of the same game (which it is). The *only* difference centers around the eligibility of the pitcher.

Pitching eligibility rules were devised to protect the health of young pitchers and these may not be violated, even in a rescheduled game. If a regulation-drawn game originally played on Wednesday is rescheduled for Saturday, and the pitcher had pitched in four innings when the game was called, he would not be eligible to pitch on Saturday. Coaches should know this, but many of them do not. It should be carefully explained to them by the umpire. Using the young pitcher could impair his health, and would result in a forfeit for having used an ineligible pitcher.

3. A suspended game. If a game has to be called before it is a regulation or a regulation-drawn game—that is, before four complete innings of play—it must be rescheduled and replayed as a complete game. It should be noted in the score book, but a new score sheet is prepared by the scorekeeper. Everything is just as if it were a new game. However, the pitching rules explained above still apply.

In a tightly scheduled season, a suspended or drawn game can create serious scheduling problems (if only the difficulty of finding a mutually open date when the field, equipment and officials are available). It is not uncommon to see a rescheduled game ready to begin with no umpires, score-keepers or equipment, as the responsible official failed to follow through on making the necessary arrangements.

The important problem, however, centers around the eligibility of the pitchers. The pitching eligibility rule was instituted for the sole purpose of protecting the physical well-

When you are umpiring behind the plate, you must be alert and keep your eyes open. Was the pitch a strike? Did the batter swing at the ball? Did the batter foul the ball? Was the batter hit by the ball?

being of the young pitcher. If a pitcher has used up his eligible innings (see page 74) during the regularly scheduled games, he cannot be used in a rescheduled game. In other words, he can pitch in the rescheduled game provided he meets the regular pitching eligibility rules. Coaches, managers and other league officials need to understand this when attempting to reach mutual agreement on the rescheduling of a regulation-drawn game or a suspended game.

Scorekeepers should be notified of the called game. If it is a regulation-drawn game, the same score sheet is used in the rescheduled game as the players (with the possible exception of the pitcher) must assume the positions they held when the game was called. This should be noted on the score sheet. If it is a suspended game, it should be so noted on the original score sheet, but a new score sheet is used in the rescheduled game, since it is a completely new ball game.

4. A forfeited game. You should make every effort to prevent any situation that might cause a game to end in a forfeiture. In some cases, however, this is not possible, so you must know what a forfeiture is and how to go about declaring one. Actually, there are some wrong notions as to what constitutes a forfeiture. The chief umpire is the only one who can declare a game forfeited, and it can be done only under the circumstances described below. When this is the case, it must be so recorded in the official score book and the umpire must sign it. The umpire must also prepare a written report stating the reason for the forfeit and file it with the president of the league within 24 hours. This is for administrative purposes only and is the proper thing to do, although failure to prepare such a report does not cancel the forfeit.

There are only four situations in which a game could be called a forfeit:

A. If a team is unable or refuses to field nine eligible uniformed players. If a team is unable to field nine eligible players within ten minutes after the umpire calls "play ball," a forfeit can be declared in favor of the team that *is* ready to play. For this reason, the umpire must be conscious of the time. Check with the manager of each team to make certain your watches are in agreement. Decide which one is the official time before the scheduled beginning of the game.

Apply the ten-minute rule understandingly. If there is reason to believe the delay was unavoidable, or if it looks like the offending team will get nine eligible players on the field within a short period of time, give them a little leeway. (Picking up an extra player who is not on the official roster of that team is not permitted at any time.) Under no circumstances should you "count down" the seconds while watching a team pile out of a station wagon and onto the playing field.

Teams must not only start by fielding nine eligible players, but they must continue to do so for the entire game. Quite frequently, teams will want to play anyway—just for the practice. There is nothing wrong with this, but you should make it perfectly clear that the game has been forfeited so that no misunderstandings can occur should the missing players arrive later and be inserted into the lineup.

In rare instances, managers refuse to field a team for one reason or another. It might be because they think the other team is using illegal equipment, or an ineligible player. None of these excuses are valid, and they may even be serving as a delaying tactic while awaiting the arrival of other team members. The umpire should quickly, kindly, but firmly explain that the penalty for such actions is forfeiture. There should be absolutely no argument on this point. The decision to declare a forfeit in this situation should take no longer than the ten-minute grace period described above and the offending parties should be made aware of it.

B. If a team uses tactics to delay or shorten a game. In many cases, Little League ball games must meet time limitations due to tightly scheduled ball parks, evening hours, and for other similar reasons. Under these circumstances, you might run into a situation where it would be to the advantage of one manager to delay the completion of a ball game. If, for example, the game is scheduled to end at 5:00 P.M., the manager of the team which is ahead might try to stall or delay the game to prevent another inning from beginning so that his team would be the winner. He might do this by asking for time frequently, making a number of substitutions,

A close play at first base demands a quick decision. Did this runner beat out the throw to first?

or asking for permission to talk with his catcher. If you suspect that this is the case, call time and warn the offending manager that he might lose the game through forfeiture. A warning is usually sufficient. However, if the delays continue be ready to take the necessary action.

A rare but possible situation might develop where the opposite action might take place; where a coach or manager would attempt to shorten a game deliberately and make it end while his team was ahead. This could also result in a forfeiture if your warnings were to go unheeded.

C. The use of an ineligible player. In any situation where a manager uses a player who is not eligible for play, the game

73

Make sure you watch the base runners to see that they tag each base. At any time before the next pitch, the fielding team may decide to appeal the run, and you will have to rule on the appeal.

can be forfeited. This is especially possible in the case of ineligible pitchers. Pitchers are limited to 6 innings per week, and if they pitch more than three innings on one day (even one pitch into the fourth inning) they must have three calendar days' rest. This is why the job of a scorekeeper is so important.

Accurate and complete records of the pitching schedules, must be kept. Most coaches know this rule and try to abide by it, but occasionally, whether intentionally or not, a coach will violate this rule. If it is violated, the game can be forfeited.

D. If a team continues to violate the rules willfully. This sometimes happens, although not very often. If a coach violates a rule and continues to do so after having been warned by the umpire, it can result in a forfeit. The threat of a forfeit is probably all that is needed to handle most situations. It is a valuable tool, and sometimes the only tool that an umpire has to enforce compliance with the rules.

Protesting a Ball Game

Protested games are messy to handle, and unfortunately there are too many of them. Even worse, most of the protests are not legitimate. Protests can be made only when they are based on a violation or misinterpretation of a playing rule, including the use of an ineligible player.

Any manager or coach can protest a game if he believes the umpire has misinterpreted a playing rule. A judgment call cannot be protested as there is absolutely no way to prove it. A foul ball, a foul tip, or a close call on a tag are judgment calls and protests on them are not possible. However, if an umpire overlooks or misinterprets a rule, a protest is in order.

Protests on all but ineligible players should be made before the next ball is pitched. Protests concerning an ineligible player must be made before the game ends. (Any ineligible player must be removed from the ball game, and the game should be continued, even if under protest.) If a manager really believes that an umpire has overlooked or misinterpreted a playing rule, time should be called and permission requested to discuss it with the umpire. After this discussion (possibly involving other umpires on the field) the chief umpire might want to reconsider the call and change the decision. *This should be done only if the umpire was wrong.*

If a manager disagrees with the umpire's final decision, and believes the umpire was wrong, an announcement must be made to the umpire that the game is being played under protest from that point. The umpire must notify the score-keeper who records it in the score book. The manager and the umpire must submit individual written statements outlining the situation within 24 hours to the league president. The league president must then assemble a committee composed of the league president, a player agent and one or more other officers of the league who are not managers, coaches or umpires, and resolve the issue. If the protest is found to be valid, the game must be replayed from the exact point of the protest—the pitching rules on eligibility being observed.

Every effort should be made to keep protests to a minimum, as they foul up the pitching and game schedules, and threaten to mock the Little League ideal of sportsmanship. In the discussions between the offended manager and the umpires, proper decorum should exist. Voices should not be raised, and tempers should not be allowed to flare. The ideal situation would be to have any possible violations brought to the attention of the offending manager before the game begins, rather than to make a spectacle as soon as the pitcher throws the first ineligible ball!

When a protest is made, the umpire should do his best to explain to the scorekeeper, the fans and the players that a misunderstanding exists, and that the game is being played under protest until the issue can be resolved. The umpire should not belittle anyone through his actions or his voice. The same goes for the managers. The American way to settle differences should not be through verbal abuse, and certainly not through any harmful physical actions.

Preventative Umpiring

There is much an umpire can do to prevent the undesirable from taking place on the field. Many problems can be prevented if the umpire knows the rules, applies them fairly, and immediately uses common sense procedures which would help avoid upsetting managers, coaches, players and fans. The whole idea is to *prevent* misunderstandings. The umpire might even take advantage of lulls in the action such as between innings, to discuss potential problems with players or managers. For instance, an umpire might casually mention to a coach that the pitcher is close to balking and suggest that it be corrected. This might prevent a balk from happening during a more crucial and lively time in the game.

In general, the umpire should give the impression of friendliness to all players, managers, and coaches, and he should never bypass the opportunity of helping a player to improve or to further the ideal of sportsmanship. However, the umpire must not assume the role of a coach, as that is not his official duty! If a situation develops where it seems desirable to discuss a problem with a player, the coach should also be informed.

Call It Right!

Situation 9: Runners are on second and third. One out. The batter hits a high fly ball to center field. The runner at third leaves the base too soon (before the ball has crossed the plate), then realizes it is a fly ball, and quickly returns to his base. The center fielder misses the ball, allowing the batter to reach first. Both runners advance, with the runner coming home from third. Does his run count? Or is he out?

Situation 10: A runner on first leaves the base too soon. The batter gets a hit into right field but the fielder cannot make a play for an out, and the runner from first gets to second base safely. Is the runner out? Or is he called back to first base?

(See page 89 for solutions.)

Troublesome Rules and Difficult Calls

Most people who watch baseball games have no trouble following the action. They know what an "out" is and what "balls" and "strikes" are—sometimes better than the umpire! They know how runners are put out on the bases, when a fly ball is fair or foul and how a game is won. They get into difficulty, however, along with many inexperienced umpires, when complicated and uncommon situations arise. Umpires only add to the confusion when they don't know the rule or how to interpret it.

Troublesome situations usually develop in several areas: the "infield fly," the "balk," "leaving the base too soon," and a few other odd situations. Throughout this book, some of these problem "game situations" were posed to stimulate your thinking, and if you have read the material in the succeeding chapters carefully, many of these situations have been clarified. What follows is designed to help you understand some other difficult rules and situations. (Even more problems are given starting on page 90.)

The Infield Fly

The "infield fly" rule is difficult for most people to understand, and many beginning umpires are uncertain in its application. See Rules 2.00, 6.05 and 7.08.

The "infield fly" rule was designed to prevent an infielder from deliberately dropping a fly ball when men are on base in order to make a double play. For example, with runners on first and second bases, a third baseman could drop an easily caught pop fly on purpose, then pick it up, step on third base for one out and then throw to second base for the second out. Had he caught the ball, only the hitter would have been out. Hence, the rule protects the offensive team against a situation where the batter would normally be out on a fly ball.

An "infield fly" ball is determined by the following conditions:

1. There must be a potential double play situation on the bases (runners on first and second, or with the bases loaded).

2. There must be less than two out.

3. The ball must be arching and be caught by infielders in their normal positions through ordinary effort.

Pitchers, catchers or outfielders who position themselves in the infield are considered "infielders" in this situation.

Understanding this, the rule makes more sense. It is an "infield fly" ball if it is in fair territory and could be easily caught by an infielder playing in his normal position (the position he occupies at the time the ball is pitched). A line drive or an attempted bunt is not an "infield fly" ball. If a batted ball arches into the air and is contained within the infield, and if there are runners on first and second, or first, second and third with less than two outs, it is an "infield fly" ball and the batter is automatically out. Runners may advance at their own risk, as with any other fly ball. The umpire should be alert and declare an "infield fly" ball as soon as possible. In cases where there is some doubt, for example, if a fly ball is dropping near the base line, the umpire should declare it an "infield fly" ball. If it drops "fair" but rolls into "foul" territory, then it is treated as any other foul ball. If the ball falls *untouched* into foul territory, but rolls fair in the infield, it is still considered an "infield fly."

Another point about the "infield fly" rule that is overlooked by many umpires and fans is that if a base runner is hit by or interferes with an infield fly he is out (as is usually the case), *but* the batter is also out.

The Balk

When a pitcher on the mound makes any movement with any part of his body toward the plate, he must have the ball in his possession and deliver it to the plate and the batter. If he does anything to make a batter or base runner think he is going to pitch the ball to the plate and doesn't, it is a "balk." See Rule 8.05. The pitcher balks if he

- delivers the ball while not facing the batter.
- delivers an illegal pitch.
- drops the ball while standing on the rubber.
- delivers the ball when the catcher is out of his box when deliberately walking a hitter.
- stands on the mound or straddles the rubber and feigns a pitch without having the ball.
- feigns a pitch to an unoccupied base.
- goes into his pitching motion and fails to deliver the ball.

The whole idea behind the balk rule is to make the pitcher deliver the ball as his intentions indicate when he gets on the mound. He cannot trick a hitter or a base runner into thinking he is going to pitch when he isn't, or do anything to distract a batter or base runner unfairly. The balk rule also gives the runner and the batter protection against an illegally thrown ball. Any movement made by the pitcher with any part of his body that he would normally use to deliver the ball to the plate *without delivering the ball* is a "balk." The penalty is severe enough that pitchers are usually very careful about learning and using the proper pitching technique. If there are runners on base when a "balk" is committed, they all advance one base, and it is neither a ball nor a strike against the hitter.

Leaving the Base Too Soon

In Little League baseball, sometimes too much emotional strain exists, and when it does, players do not enjoy the game as much as they should. One of these pressure situations occurs when there are runners on base. This puts more pressure on the pitcher, catcher and the infield than is felt justified, and taxes players who are not yet able to handle the stolen-base and lead-off situations. This can easily lead to frustration.

To compensate for these pressures, a rule was established to make the situation more fair to offensive as well as defensive players. Rule 7.13 is patterned after the one in softball, and simply states that base runners may not leave a base until after the pitched ball crosses the plate. This is simple enough to understand and not difficult to detect.

Detection is a matter of judgment, just as in many other baseball calls. However, an umpire can be quite objective and accurate if he learns to watch the feet of base runners and the flight of the ball simultaneously. When the rule has been violated, the umpire simply drops a handkerchief or a cloth marker (preferably red), and, after the play is over, tells the runner to return to the nearest unoccupied base or the one he left.

The interpretation of this rule begins to get a little sticky when the batter gets a hit, since it is generally felt that the batter must not be penalized for the actions of runners in front of him if they leave the bases too soon. The situation becomes even more critical when the runner is on third base, and his would be the winning run. This is not an impossible situation. On more than one occasion, a runner who left third base too soon was not seen by the umpire! This should not be allowed to happen. The third-base umpire should watch the runner at third base and not the hitter. He should have dropped his flag immediately and made the necessary decision.

When interpreting the base-running rule and assessing the penalty, the following must be kept in mind:

1. The hitter must not be penalized for the infractions committed by his teammate runners ahead of him. If the bases are loaded and any runner leaves too soon *and* the hitter gets a home run, all runs score and the batter should get credit for the runs batted in.

Example: Bases loaded, runner on third leaves too soon and batter gets a base on balls. Runner from third will be allowed to score, and batter is credited with a run batted in.

2. A runner who leaves the base too soon must return to that base, *if it is an open base.* Obviously, a runner can't return to the base if it has been occupied as a result of a legally batted ball.

Example: Runner on second base leaves too soon. Batter gets a single. Runner must return to second.

3. No run shall be allowed to score on an infield hit when any runner leaves the base too soon.

Example: The bases are loaded and the batter gets to first safely on an infield hit. The runner on third base is not called out. His run is not allowed to score—he is simply removed from the field.

4. If a runner leaves the base too soon and is thrown out, the "out" stands. The runner advances at his own risk.

Example: A runner on second leaves too soon, is tagged out at third and the batter hits safely to first base. The runner advanced at his own risk, and the "out" stands.

Spectator Interference

When a spectator interferes with a thrown or batted ball, it affects both the defensive and the offensive players. If a "spectator," such as a bat boy, a water boy, an umpire, or coach who is authorized to be inside the ball park interferes intentionally with a batted or thrown ball, the ball is declared "dead" and no runners may advance. If it is accidental, the ball is "alive" and play continues. In these situations, the umpire must determine if the act was intentional or accidental.

In the case of the spectator or "fan" so near the playing field that interference is possible (this happens in some ball parks where the front row of bleachers is next to the fence), different rules must apply. If a spectator interferes with a thrown or batted ball in such a way as to prevent the defensive player from making a play, the penalty goes against the offensive player. On the other hand, if the interference prevents the offensive player from getting a hit or an extra base when the defensive player is not involved, the penalty goes against the defensive player. Here are some examples:

● A fan leans over the fence and deflects or catches a ball, preventing the defensive player from making the catch. The penalty goes against the offensive player. In this case the hitter would be out.

● A fan reaches up and catches a batted ball as it goes over the fence in fair territory. The hitter would be awarded a "home run," as obviously it would have been a home run had the fan not caught it.

● A fan leans over the center field fence and catches or deflects a batted ball from the fielder's mitt. This penalty would then go against the batter who would be declared out and all runners would be required to return to the bases they occupied before the batter hit the ball.

● A fan leans over the center field fence to catch a batted ball which would have dropped against the fence, out of reach of the center fielder. In this case the umpire would award the batter a double and all runners are allowed to advance as far as the "double" would have normally permitted. In all cases, where an "unauthorized" fan touches the ball, the umpire must call it a dead ball, and then assess the penalties as the situation may dictate.

Call It Right!

Now that you have learned some of the peculiar and least understood rules and their intent, let's see how well you can interpret them. The following solutions are for the situations posed throughout the book at the beginning of each chapter and there are additional situations and solutions for you to think about. Read each one, think carefully, and call it right!

Situation 1 Solution: The pitcher must have the ball in his possession when he is on the mound ready to pitch. This would be considered a balk and all runners would advance one base. The balk could be called even if the pitcher stood straddling the rubber. All efforts have been made to take trickery out of Little League play and to make it equally fair to offense and defense. Rule 8.05.

Situation 2 Solution: The ball then becomes a foul ball and the umpire must reverse his decision. Rule 2.00.

Situation 3 Solution: This is a balk on the pitcher unless the batter had deliberately tried to cause the pitcher to balk. This could have been done deliberately to walk in a winning run from third base. Rules 8.05 and 4.06 (3).

The first thing an umpire should do is to call "time out" to give the situation careful consideration. It is difficult to determine if such an action was deliberate. He might ask the hitter, or he might ask the manager, but this usually provides no conclusive answer. Unless the umpire overheard instructions being given to the hitter, intention is difficult to

Move quickly into proper position to make the call at first base. This umpire is ready to call it right.

prove. About all an umpire can do is consult his other umpires and then make a decision.

Situation 4 Solution: He should rule that this cannot be done. It would place the right fielder in foul territory, and only the catcher can be stationed in foul territory. Rule 4.03.

Situation 5 Solution: Only an umpire can call "time." The coach or manager can only request it. Rule 5.10.

Situation 6 Solution: The opposing coach is right. The rule book limits the number of times a coach may visit with his pitcher in any given inning to three. The third trip to the same pitcher necessitates the removal of the pitcher. The reason for this rule is to help prevent deliberate attempts to slow down the game. It also helps to mitigate the dominance of the game by an adult. Rule 8.06.

Situation 7 Solution: The umpire should instruct the score-keeper to mind his own business!!! This is not the prerogative of the scorekeeper. The only way this hitter should be called out is through an appeal by the opposing coach who, through a properly called time out, draws it to the attention of the chief umpire. The umpire must then check with the scorekeeper to confirm the appeal. Most scorekeepers in Little League are fathers, mothers, brothers or sisters of players and get a little too anxious to call an out on the opposing team. It is the responsibility of the chief umpire to make certain scorekeepers are aware of this rule and know their proper place. Rule 6.07.

Situation 8 Solution: The umpire should stop the game. It is obviously too dark to play, and to continue to do so would expose the players to unnecessary injury. The game has gone less than four complete innings, so it would not be a regulation game. It must be called a "no game" or "suspended game" and replayed at a later date. Rules 4.10(d) and 2.00.

Situation 9 Solution: Many people criticize the rule that governs this situation, but actually it is a good one for Little League players. Staying on the base until after the ball has crossed the plate really doesn't detract much from the game and it takes some of the emotional pressure off the pitcher and catcher as well as from the defensive players.

When interpreting Rule 7.13 it would be helpful to remember that the batter is not the one to be penalized and that a runner cannot be made to return to a base if all the bases behind him are legally occupied.

With runners on second and third, a single would normally score the runner from third. However, since the runner at third left too soon, both he and the runner who advanced from second to third are required to return to the bases they left, as both would be unoccupied.

The complicating factor in this situation is the fact that the runner on third, having realized that he left the base too soon, retraced his steps and still had time to reach home. Many umpires erroneously allow the run to count. The run cannot count! The runner broke the rule and must pay the penalty—which is to return to the base unless it is legally occupied.

If the batter had gotten a double, it would score the runner from third and the runner advancing from second would be required to remain on or return to third base.

Situation 10 Solution: Refer back to *Situation 9* for the background for this. Another thing to take into consideration on a play like this one is that the batter should not be penalized for the actions of the runner in front of him if he leaves the base too soon. Should the runner be required to return to first base, where would the batter who hit the ball cleanly be allowed to go? He has nowhere to go. The runner would not be out. He would be permitted to advance at his own risk. If he were thrown out at second, that out would stand, but he is otherwise allowed to remain on second base. Had the runner ended up on third, he would be required to return to second base. Rule 7.13.

Situation 11: With a runner on first, the batter hits the ball sharply to the outfield. The center fielder moves toward the ball and attempts to catch it. It strikes his glove and bounces over the fence without having touched the ground. Is it a double? Is it a home run? Or is the runner at first base allowed to score?

Solution: It is a home run. All runners on base may score. In this situation the ball is so close to the fence it might have gone over anyway. Rule 6.09. If, in the opinion of the umpire, the ball would not have gone over the fence, and was less than 165 feet from home plate, it would not be a home run and the batter would only be entitled to two bases.

Situation 12: There is a water-filled hole in short right field. A ball is hit between first and second base and bounces into the water-filled hole. The fielder slips down trying to field it. How far are the runners permitted to advance?

Solution: This situation should never be permitted to develop! It is an unsafe condition and the chief umpire should not have permitted the game to begin until the hole was filled. However, in the event that this repair is impossible, the umpire should, in consultation with other league officials present and the manager of both teams involved, establish a "ground rule" before the game begins to cover this situation. To be fair to all concerned, this ground rule should prevent the runner from advancing beyond the base toward which he is running. If no ground rule had been established, the ball would be live and playable.

Situation 13: There is no one on first or third, but there is a runner on second base who leaves too soon. The hitter gets a clean single into right field. The hitter gets to first safely, and the runner on second gets safely to third. Should he be called back to second or should he be permitted to remain on third?

Solution: The runner must return to second base. Had the hitter gotten a double, the runner advancing to third would be permitted to remain there. In that situation, to have the runner return to second would force the hitter to return to first, and thus rob him of a double. Rule 7.13.

Situation 14: A runner on second base attempts to steal third after the pitch crosses the plate. He runs into the third baseman, who has the ball ready to make the tag. The resulting collision knocks the third baseman out, and the ball dribbles into the third base dugout. The runner goes on to score. Does his run count? Or is he made to return to third?

Solution: Yes, the run counts, but, as soon as play is ended, the umpire should call "time," in which case the ball would be dead. Any other men on base could, before time is called, advance one base. Rule 5.10.

Situation 15: The batter hits the ball, which then hits the dirt between home plate and the batter's box. The batter gets to first base as the catcher fields the ball on or in front of the plate and holds it. Is it a fair ball? Does the runner stay on first base?

Solution: The area between the batter's box and home plate itself is in "fair territory," and a ball hitting home plate is not a dead ball, but playable. The batter is awarded a single.

Situation 16: A runner advancing from second to third is struck by the batted ball, and the hitter gets to first base safely. Is he permitted to remain there? And will the runner who was hit by the ball be permitted to go to third base?

Solution: This is called "interference." The ball is dead if it is deflected or stopped by a runner before it passes or touches an infielder. Under these conditions, it would "interfere" with the infielder trying to make a play on the ball, and the penalty for this action is an out on the runner. Rule 7.08 (f). It makes no difference if the interference is accidental, as the umpire has no way of knowing this. However, the penalty could be even more severe: the batter could also be called out if the "infield fly" rule were in effect.

Situation 17: After a batter takes one swing at the pitched ball, the opposing coach calls "time out" and demands that, since the player has turned 13 years of age over the weekend, he is ineligible to play. Should the umpire remove the player from the game?

Solution: Players cannot turn 13 during the playing season, and all birthdays must be accurately checked by League officials before the season begins. Hence, this must be considered a delaying tactic on the part of the opposing coach and the game should continue with the player in the line-up. The opposing coach should be given the opportunity to protest the game, and the issue would be settled later by League officials.

Situation 18: The score is tied at 0–0 at the end of the fourth inning, and the umpire "calls" the game because of darkness. Does the game have to be played over?

Solution: No. After a game has gone four innings, it must be continued from that point at the later date until one team has scored more runs than the other in an equal number of innings. The pitcher would continue pitching, provided he still meets the eligibility requirements. Rule 4.11 (e).

Situation 19: After the fourth inning, one team leads the other by a score of 20–5. The umpire "calls" the game, saying that the one team was 10 runs or more ahead and declares that team the winner. Can he do this?

Solution: No, not unless there has been an agreement before the game begins, or if the local league has established such a ruling. There is no such rule in Little League baseball.

Situation 20: With a runner on first base, the next hitter belts the ball to the fence line. Just as the ball nears the fence, a spectator attempts to catch it, and it drops inside the fence into the playing area. What is the correct ruling? Is it a home run? Do both runs score?

Solution: The ball would be declared dead the moment the spectator touched it. The batter would be out and the runners should not advance. If it is clearly over the fence it is a home run and all runs would score. Rule 3.16.

Situation 21: With a runner on second base, the hitter gets a home run. However, the runner on second base leaves the base too soon. Do both runs count?

Solution: The batter should not be penalized for the actions of any base runners ahead of him. Any base runners ahead of this batter would have scored on the home run anyway. In this case, the run would be allowed to stand as the runner would otherwise be required to return to second. If the batter hit a double, the runner would be allowed to go only to third. A home run or a triple would clear the bases and the batter should get credit for all the runs batted in. Rule 7.13 (7).

Situation 22: A game is being played under a "time limit" to clear the ball park for the next game. The manager of the visiting team, realizing that he is ahead, thinks if he could delay the game long enough to prevent the next inning from starting, he could win the game. Consequently he changes catchers, having them take as much time as possible to change their protective equipment. He later calls "time" and asks permission to talk with his center fielder. What should be the umpires' instructions to him?

Solution: The coach is obviously trying to delay the game so he can win. He should be warned when he starts that his delaying tactics will result in a forfeiture, and the warning should be carried out. Rule 4.15.

Situation 23: On a close call at first base, an umpire calls the runner out as he tries to beat out a ground ball. The player's manager immediately calls for time and tells the umpire: "This game is being played under protest from this point." The umpire then goes to the scorekeeper and informs him or her that the game is being played under protest. Is this the correct procedure?

Solution: No. The manager is out of order. Only those calls which are in violation of a playing rule can be protested. A "judgment" call such as this cannot be protested, or the League would be tied up in protests all season. Rule 4.19 (a).

Situation 24: At 5:00 P.M., the time the game was scheduled to begin, the umpire calls "play ball." One team has only eight eligible players on the field. What action does the umpire take?

Solution: First of all he must make certain that his watch is correct and then be patient. This is not a hard and fast rule. The object of the game is to play ball, not forfeit. If the team arrives at the ball park just as the second hand on the clock shows that ten minutes have passed, the game should still be permitted to continue. If, of course, the team cannot be seen anywhere, or the ninth man is not going to be there, a forfeit should be called. Rule 4.15.

Situation 25: The runner on first base attempts to steal second, and as the catcher makes the throw to second base, the umpire accidentally touches the glove of the catcher, causing his throw to be wild. Is the runner required to return to first?

Solution: The runner is required to return to first base and the ball is dead. Rule 5.09 (b).

Situation 26: An umpire gives a manager permission for a "time out," whereupon he calls for his center fielder to come to the foul line for a discussion. Is this permitted?

Solution: This is not permitted. The only defensive player the manager is permitted to talk to while the game is in progress is the pitcher. The catcher may be present, but the manager cannot call time out to talk with any other player. Rule 8.06.

Index

adults, handling, 64–65
athletic supporter, 37
atmosphere of game, 59

balk, 25, 81–82
ball sack, 16
balls and strikes, 21–23,
    35–38
base-running rule, 83–84
batting order, 59, 67
before the game, 59–62
broom, 14

calls, 21–31
    at plate, 39–42
    troublesome, 79–85
character of the umpire,
    9–10
checking a swing, 41
chest protector, 15–16
chief umpire, 33–42
    plus one, 42–50
    plus three, 55–57
    plus two, 50–54
coaches, handling, 64–65
command post, 34
conference, confidential,
    34
control, loss of, 36–37
corners of plate, 36–37
counter, balls-and-strikes,
    14
covering first and third,
    42
cup and supporter, 37

dead ball, 30
delaying tactics, 72–73
dependability, 10–13
difficult calls, 79–85
dress standards, 13

eligible players, 71–72
ending a ball game, 68–75
equipment, 14–16

face mask, 14
fair or foul ball, 28, 38–39
fans, handling, 65–66
field decorum, 59–77
firmness, friendliness and
    fairness, 17–18
flag, 30
forfeited game, 71
foul or fair ball, 28, 38–39
foul tip, 29
full count, 38

ground rules, 62–63

hand signals, 21–31
hot-box, 47, 54, 55

impartiality, 17–18
ineligible player, 73–75
infield fly, 79–81
interference, 26,
    spectator, 84–85

knowledge and training,
    18–19

leaving the base too soon,
    30, 82–84
loss of control, 36–37

mask, 14

obstruction, 26
out, 23–25

percentage play, 42, 44,
    45, 47
pick-off play, 49
plate, calls at the, 39–42
plate umpire, 33
players, 63–64, 71–72,
    73–75
positioning and responsi-
    bility, 33–57

positions, normal, 43, 45,
    46, 50–53, 54, 55
pre-game preparations,
    11, 59, 60, 61, 62–63
preventative umpiring, 77
protests, 75–76

regulation-drawn game,
    68–69
regulation game, 68
roster and batting order,
    59, 67
rules, violation, 75
    troublesome, 79–85

safe, 25
scorebook, 67, 69, 70–71,
    76
scorekeepers, 66–67
sex barrier, 19
shin guards, 16
shortening tactics, 72–73
signals, hand, 21–31
situations and solutions,
    8, 20, 32, 58, 78, 86–95
spectator interference,
    84–85
strikes and balls, 21–23,
    35–38
superintending the game,
    33–35
suspended game, 69–71

ten-minute rule, 71–72
time, 25
training, 18–19
troublesome rules, 79–85

umpire, 9–19
umpires' school, 19
umpire's signals, 21–30

violations, willful, 75
voice of the umpire, 21

walk, 30–31
whisk broom, 14